Free time

1

Describing likes and dislikes

1 **Read. Who likes sports?**

_____ likes sports.

Hi! My name's Kate and I'm 9 years old. I'm from Ireland. I like watching TV and playing computer games. *Fashion Queen* is my favourite computer game. It's really cool! I also like singing and dancing with my friends at parties. My friends think I'm a very good dancer. I don't like cleaning and I don't like cooking. My sister and my mum like cooking. I don't – but I like eating!

Hello! I'm Santiago and I'm from Argentina. I'm 10 years old. I like playing football in the park with my friends. I also like skateboarding and skiing. Sports are great! I like reading sports magazines too. My brother doesn't like sports – he likes watching TV and surfing the Internet. I don't like watching TV and I don't like surfing the Internet. They're boring!

2 **Read again. Then circle _T_ (True) or _F_ (False).**

1 Kate is from Argentina.   T /(F)
2 She likes playing computer games.   T / F
3 She doesn't like dancing.   T / F
4 Kate's sister likes cooking   T / F
5 Santiago is 10.   T / F
6 He doesn't like skiing.   T / F
7 He likes watching TV.   T / F
8 Santiago's brother likes surfing the Internet.   T / F

1 Leisure activities

3 **Read. Then match.**

1 surfing   a TV
2 reading   b the guitar
3 watching   c the Internet
4 playing   d online
5 walking   e the newspaper
6 chatting   f the dog

4 **Find four more activities.**

decleaningbaskiingerskateboardingmoskippingsicookinged

5 **Write *a*, *e*, *i* or *o*. Then number.**

a

1 pl_a_y_i_ng h_o_ck_e_y
2 p_ _ _nt_ng
3 sk_pp_ng
4 w_tch_ng f_lms
5 c_ _k_ng
6 r_ _d_ng m_g_z_n_s

b

c  1

d

e

f

Remember!

I like playing computer games.

I don't like riding a scooter.

6 Write three things you like doing and three things you don't like doing.

I like ...	I don't like ...

7 Write about the things you like and don't like doing.
Then write about a friend.

<u>Me</u>

My name is _____
and I'm _____ years old. I like
_____
_____
_____
_____
_____
_____
_____

<u>My friend</u>

My friend's name is _____
and he/she is _____ years old.
_____ likes _____
_____
_____
_____
_____
_____
_____

2 Wild animals

Describing animals

1 Read. Then circle.

Tigers
by Steve Smith

Tigers are very big cats. They live in the jungle and they eat meat. They're big and strong. They've got black and orange stripes, sharp teeth and sharp claws. They can run very fast and they can swim well. They like water – they often swim when it's hot. There aren't any tigers in my country but there's a zoo near my house. It's got three big tigers and some cute tiger cubs too. They're amazing!

Zebras
by Maria Alvarez

Zebras live in grasslands in Africa. They look like horses and they've got black and white stripes. Zebras are herbivores: they eat grass, leaves and fruit. They eat during the day and sleep at night. Zebras can hear very well and they can also see well at night. They can run fast too. Baby zebras are amazing.They can walk when they are 20 minutes old! And they can run when they are only 1 hour old!

1 Tigers live in *grasslands /* (*the jungle*).

2 They *can / can't* run fast.

3 They *like / don't like* water.

4 Zebras are *carnivores / herbivores*.

5 They *eat / sleep* at night.

2 Read again. Then answer.

1 What do tigers eat?   They eat meat.

2 Do they swim well? _____

3 Where do zebras live? _____

4 What do they eat? _____

5 Do they hear well? _____

3 Write.

1 zebra   **2** _____   **3** _____

4 _____   **5** _____   **6** _____

4 Write. Use words from the box.

| camel crocodile giraffe hippo panda ~~tiger~~ |

1 I've got orange and black stripes.   tiger

2 I'm tall and I eat leaves.   _____

3 I live in rivers and I've got a long tail.   _____

4 I live in deserts and I walk slowly.   _____

5 I'm big and grey and I like water.   _____

6 I'm black and white and I live in forests.   _____

5 Match the two parts of the words.

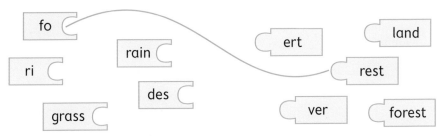

2 Describing animals

6 Think of two animals. Write notes.

Animal:		Animal:	
Lives:		Lives:	
Eats:		Eats:	
Has got:		Has got:	
Can:		Can:	
Can't:		Can't:	

7 Write about the animals from Activity 6.

The seasons

Describing the weather

1 **What's the weather like today where you live? Write.**

_____

2 **Read. Then write the temperatures.**

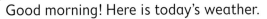

Good morning! Here is today's weather.

Here in the north it's cloudy with some rain and a temperature of 21 degrees. In the west it's very hot and humid – the temperature is 35 degrees! Now let's look at the south. There are lots of clouds in the south today. But it isn't cold – the temperature is 24 degrees. And now the east: there's a lot of rain and wind. The temperature is 20 degrees. Don't forget your umbrella!

1 north: _____twenty-one_____ degrees

2 west: _____ degrees

3 south: _____ degrees

4 east: _____ degrees

3 **Read again. Then circle _T_ (True) or _F_ (False).**

1 It's sunny in the north.   T / F⃝

2 It's wet and windy in the west.   T / F

3 There's thunder and lightning in the west.   T / F

4 There are a lot of clouds in the south.   T / F

5 It's rainy in the east.   T / F

4 **Unscramble. Find the seasons.**

1 inetrw   _w i n t e r_   2 auumtn   _ _ _ _ _ _ _

3 srpign   _ _ _ _ _ _ _   4 rsemum   _ _ _ _ _ _ _

5 **Match the two parts of the words.**

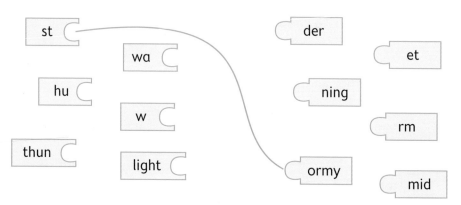

st	wa	der
hu	w	et
thun	light	ning
		rm
	ormy	mid

6 **Write a, e, i or o.**

1 g**o** w**a**t**e**r sk**i i**ng

2 g_ c_mp_ng

3 g_ sn_wb_ _rd_ng

4 g_ h_k_ng

Remember!

Some words have a silent letter.

autumn   column

7 **What can you do? Write two activities for each season.**

1 autumn: _____

2 winter: _____

3 spring: _____

4 summer: _____

8 **Write about today's weather.**

- What's the weather like?
- What's the temperature?
- What activities can / can't you do?

4 My week

A timetable

1 Look at Rosa's timetable and underline five more mistakes.

	Morning	Afternoon
MON	study English (9.15–11.30)	practise the piano (2.15–3.15)
TUES	study English (9.15–11.30)	have ballet lessons (3.00–4.00)
WED	study English (9.15–11.30)	practise the piano (2.30–3.30)
THURS	study English (9.15–11.30)	have ballet lessons (2.45–3.45)
FRI	study English (9.15–11.30)	do gymnastics (4.00–5.00)
SAT	do karate (10.00–11.00)	practise the piano (3.15–4.00)

1 On Mondays Rosa practises the piano at <u>half past two</u>.

2 On Tuesdays she has a ballet lesson at four o'clock.

3 On Wednesdays she practises the piano at a quarter to two.

4 On Thursdays she studies Maths in the morning.

5 On Fridays she does gymnastics at three o'clock.

6 On Saturdays she does karate in the afternoon.

2 Correct the mistakes in Activity 1.

1 <u>On Mondays Rosa practises the piano at a quarter past two.</u>

2 _____

3 _____

4 _____

5 _____

6 _____

3 **Write. Use words from the box.**

| ~~ballet lessons~~ | English | gymnastics | the violin | karate |
| Maths | music lessons | the piano | | |

have	do	practise	study
ballet lessons			

4 **Write. Use words from Activity 3.**

1

2

3

have ballet lessons

4

5

6

5 **Draw the time.**

1

It's half
past three.

2

It's a quarter
past twelve.

3

It's nine
o'clock.

4

It's a quarter
to seven.

4 A timetable

6 **Make your own timetable.**

	Morning	Afternoon
MON		
TUES		
WED		
THURS		
FRI		

7 **Look at Activity 6 and write about your week.**

I have a busy week. On Mondays I

1 **What do you want to be when you're older? Write.**

_____

2 **Read. Then answer.**

Dear Uncle Rob,

I'm writing to see if you can help me. At school we are doing a project on different jobs. We choose a job and then visit someone to find out about it.

I want to be a chef so I want to find out what a chef does. I want to know what time a chef gets up in the morning and starts work. Does the chef buy all the food? Can I come to your restaurant one morning next week and talk to the chef? I've got lots of questions to ask!

Thank you, Jason

1 Who is Jason writing to?

He's writing to his Uncle Rob.

2 Why is he writing the email?

_____

3 What's his school project about?

_____

4 What does he want to be?

_____

5 When does he want to go to the restaurant?

_____

5 Jobs

3 **Write. Use words from the box.**

| astronaut | ~~ballet dancer~~ | doctor |
| journalist | lawyer | police officer |

1 <u>ballet dancer</u>

2 _____

3 _____

4 _____

5 _____

6 _____

4 **Unscramble. Then write.**

1 sgneir <u>s i n g e r</u>

2 rfmare _ _ _ _ _ _

3 firifergthe _ _ _ _ _ _ _ _ _ _ _

4 fmli satr _ _ _ _ _ _ _ _

5 **Write the jobs. What's the secret word?**

1 I fix cars.

2 I take photos.

3 I build houses.

4 I work with wood.

5 I train and listen to my coach.

			1	m	e	c	h	a	n	i	c
2	p		o		o		r			e	
3		u					r				
4			r			n					
5	a						e				

Secret word: _____

Remember!

We use **a** before nouns that begin with a consonant: a builder
We use **an** before nouns that begin with a vowel: an athlete

6 **Read. Then match.**

1 Dear   a Nick

2 I want to be   b visit your hospital?

3 Can I   c Aunt Kate,

4 Thank you,   d a doctor.

7 **Read the email on page 13 and imagine you are doing the same project. Then write an email to ask someone for help.**

- Who are you writing to?

- What job do you want to ask about?

- What do you want to know?

- Where do you want to go? When?

6 In the rainforest

An article

1 Read. Then circle *T* (True) or *F* (False).

THE AMAZON RAINFOREST

by Bobby Jones

The Amazon Rainforest is the largest rainforest in the world. It's in South America. More than half of the rainforest is in Brazil. It takes its name from the river that runs through it: the Amazon River. The Amazon is the second longest river in the world.

It's called a rainforest because it rains a lot! It rains every day, usually in the afternoon. In the Amazon the rainy season is between December and May. The dry season is from June until November but there's still rain!

There are a lot of plants and animals in the Amazon Rainforest. Scientists use some of the plants for medicines, to keep us healthy. The Amazon Rainforest is a very important! We must protect it!

1 The Amazon Rainforest is in South Africa.	*T / F*
2 It takes its name from a river.	*T / F*
3 The Amazon River is the longest river in the world.	*T / F*
4 It doesn't rain very often in the Amazon Rainforest.	*T / F*
5 The rainy season starts in June.	*T / F*
6 There's still rain in the dry season.	*T / F*
7 A lot of animals live in the rainforest.	*T / F*

2 **Write. Use words from the box.**

| bridge | ~~hut~~ | lake | nest | vines | waterfall |

1 _____hut_____ **2** _____ **3** _____

4 _____ **5** _____ **6** _____

3 **Match.**

1 through

2 across

3 towards

4 around

a

b

c

d

4 **Read. Then circle.**

1 a bird with a long tail and colourful feathers: _tapir_ / (_parrot_)

2 a very big, scary spider: _crocodile_ / _giant tarantula_

3 an animal with a short neck and big ears: _tapir_ / _giraffe_

4 a very small bird: _hummingbird_ / _parrot_

6 An article

5 **Think of a place in your country. Write notes.**

Name of place:	
Where it is:	
Things to see:	
Things to do:	
Other information:	

6 **Write an article about the place from Activity 5.**

Feelings 7

A review

1 **Read. Does the writer like *Feelings*? Why?**

Feelings: A school musical

Feelings is the new play from Kidstown Primary School. And it's fantastic!

It starts when a group of children go on a journey. They want to go by plane but things go wrong! They miss the plane and instead they go by train, boat and car!

It's a great story and it can make you feel lots of different things. There are times when the children are worried and others when they are angry. There are other moments when everyone is happy and excited. There are also one or two moments when the children are sad.

When you are watching, you may ask yourself, 'Why am I smiling?' or 'Why am I crying or laughing so much?' This play has a little bit of everything! You really must go and see it.

2 **Read again. Then circle.**

1 *Feelings* is a *film /* play.

2 The story is about *a group of children / Kidstown Primary School.*

3 The children want to travel by *boat / plane.*

4 They miss their *plane / train.*

5 They *are / aren't* always happy and excited.

6 *Feelings* can make you feel *embarrassed / sad.*

③ Find and circle. Then write.

O	D	Y	A	W	N	I	N	G
S	H	Z	L	V	A	G	S	M
S	H	O	U	T	I	N	G	S
C	R	Y	I	N	G	T	R	M
U	S	G	F	I	G	P	V	I
E	T	F	G	C	I	I	L	L
S	Q	D	S	K	O	P	N	I
O	P	Y	N	T	O	I	X	N
J	S	H	A	K	I	N	G	G

1 I'm _____smiling_____ because I'm happy.

2 I'm _____ because I'm very cold.

3 I'm _____ because I'm tired.

4 I'm _____ because I'm sad.

5 I'm _____ because they can't hear me.

④ Unscramble and write. Then number.

a

b

1 smabrarsdee   <u>e m b a r r a s s e d</u>

2 poudr   _ _ _ _ _

3 noevrsu   _ _ _ _ _ _ _

4 raexdle   _ _ _ _ _ _ _

5 ereielvd   _ _ _ _ _ _ _ _

c

d

e

Remember!

We usually use capital letters for titles of books, shows, films and plays.

Danny the **C**hampion of the **W**orld
The **W**izard of **O**z

5 **Write a review of a show / play / film you like.**

- What's its name?
- What's it about?
- What's the story?
- Who's in it?

- Where are the people?
- How does it make you feel?
- Why do you like it?

8 Action!

A blog

1 Read. Where are the children going to go?

Alberto is _____.

Carla is _____.

Alberto's blog

I'm so excited! In August we're going to go to Wales. It's going to be the perfect holiday! I'm going to go sailing and fishing with my grandad and snorkelling with my sister. We're both very fond of it. I want to go scuba diving too but my dad says I can't because I'm very young. I'm also going to go surfing. My cousin Pete is going to be there and we're going to go together. It's going to be so much fun!

Alberto 10, England

Carla's blog

I'm going to go to Scotland in June and I'm really happy! My cousins live there and we're going to do lots of things together! We're going to go horse-riding. I love it because it makes me feel very relaxed. My sister's bored with horse-riding so she isn't going to come. But we're all going to go rock climbing and hang gliding – with our parents, of course! There are a lot of beautiful places there so we are also going to go hiking. It's going to be fantastic!

Carla 10, South Africa

2 Read again. Then write A (Alberto) or C (Carla).

1	fishing	A	2	sailing	
3	hang gliding		4	hiking	
5	horse-riding		6	snorkelling	
7	rock climbing		8	surfing	

3 Read. Then write.

Across ⇨
2 You wear riding ___boots___ when you go horse-riding.
4 You do this under water: _____ diving.
6 You do this on fast rivers: _____ .
8 You need a _____ when you go kayaking.

Down ⇩
1 You need a fishing _____ to go fishing.
3 You need a _____ to go surfing.
5 When you go _____ jumping, you need a long rope.
7 You wear a life _____ when you go sailing.

Crossword grid:
- 2 Across: b o o t s
- 1, 3, 4, 5, 6, 7, 8 (empty cells)

4 Unscramble. Then write.

1 eskngroliln
   s n o r k e l l i n g

2 kkaaigyn
   _ _ _ _ _ _ _

3 cbeha bvayollell
   _ _ _ _ _   _ _ _ _ _ _ _ _

4 nrfaitg
   _ _ _ _ _ _ _

5 sorhe-dirngi
   _ _ _ _ _ - _ _ _ _ _

6 fsnrigu
   _ _ _ _ _ _ _

8 A blog

5 **Pretend you are going to go on the perfect holiday. Write about it on your blog.**

- Where are you going to go? When?
- What activities are you going to do?
- Who are you going to do them with?
- How do these activities make you feel?

blog ✕

_____